W9-CQJ-229

I love learning new things about worship, and because of that, I loved reading this brilliant book. Darren and Chris take us deep into the meaning of the ancient word for "praise" and along the way they illuminate, inform and inspire us. It's essential that we worship God with understanding, and therefore this is an important book. Read it—it's time to join the Holy Roar!

—**Matt Redman**, Worship Leader & Songwriter

Chris and Darren have written an inspiring, insightful and practical book on worship. They unpack key biblical terms and, in doing so, unlock spiritual truths. Their teaching will activate within you a desire to turn your heart toward God more frequently and passionately. What could be greater than that?

—**Max Lucado**, Author & Pastor

If there's a textbook for "Praise and Worship 101", this is it. Incredibly straightforward and simultaneously profound, Darren and Chris have woven teaching and testimony together to create a practical and far-reaching framework for a language that we often strain to find words to describe. In a world that is struggling to retain its wonder and sense of awe, I highly recommend this book to the church leader and churchgoer alike.

—**Matt Maher**, Worship Leader & Songwriter

In Holy Roar, my dear friends, Chris Tomlin and Darren Whitehead do a deep dive into the historic meaning of the word "Praise". As I turned each page, my heart was freshly inspired again to worship our great God with everything I have! The scriptures challenge us to worship in spirit and in truth—this book helped me to do both!

—**Michael W. Smith**, Artist & Songwriter

Holy Roar is a very important book in this season in history. As we witness God's glory rise across the earth, Isaiah 61 tells us that His praise will burst forth like a clarion call, crossing over all our preferences and denominational barriers. I believe this book will help the greater church become rich in understanding, as the Holy Spirit leads us to live authentic, purposed, worshipful lives before our gracious and loving God. To Him be all the glory!

—**Darlene Zschech**, Worship Leader & Songwriter

Wow! There is so much packed into this book. So many great stories and Bible!! I will be reading this one over and over again. What a great tool for all of us. We will definitely be including this as curriculum in our worship university.

—**Brian Johnson**, Worship Leader & Songwriter, Bethel Music

It's so exciting to think about the people of God getting a hold of this book! What an amazing invitation to uncover the transforming language of our personal praise to God. Whether we are alone with Him in the quiet or gathered corporately, these words are going to change us forever!

—**Nathan and Christy Nockels**, Music producer; Songwriters & Worship Leaders

God has blessed Chris Tomlin and he is for many, "America's worship leader". Now, in addition to his amazing song writing and performing he has a new book out on a subject he knows well . . . worship! It's called *Holy Roar*. Written with Darren Whitehead, *Holy Roar* packed with fresh insights and illuminating stories, this book will change the way you worship.

—**Greg Laurie**, Pastor & Author

Holy Roar is such a timely book! Darren and Chris allow God to speak to our souls by teaching and reminding us "why" and "how" God calls us to worship him.

—**Jon Reddick**, Worship Leader & Songwriter

The greatest privilege we have in life is to give ourselves in worship to God. Our highest calling is to bring the gift of praise to Him. Both Darren Whitehead and Chris Tomlin have greatly impacted my personal worship and I am grateful that they continue to call us to a greater level of praise by expanding our understanding of what praise is. In a powerful yet practical revelation of worship, Holy Roar ignites a passion in us to fulfill our greatest calling. My prayer for the church is that God would awaken our hearts to surrender everything as we lift up our voices and declare the greatness of God. I believe this book will play a major role in the church's understanding of worship in years to come.

—**Banning Liebscher**, Jesus Culture Founder and Pastor,
Author of *Rooted: The Hidden Places Where God Develops You*

Holy Roar is a worship instrument! The compelling & Christ centered truths found in this book will lead you to deeper praise and equip you to lead others as well.

—**David Nasser**, Pastor & Author

Imagine the difference between playing 18 holes of golf with only one putter and then being handed a whole bag of custom golf-clubs. In this book Chris and Darren will open your eyes to all that you have at your disposal when it comes to worship. They will help you see that you don't just have to settle for a one-size-fits-all approach because you can learn to select the appropriate tool for what you are facing today. Holy Roar will help take your praise game from mini-golf to the Masters!

—**Levi Lusko**, Pastor & Author

Holy Roar gives incredibly fresh and actionable revelation for a more complete understanding of the different ways we can connect with God through our praise and worship.

—**Chris McClarney**, Worship Leader, Jesus Culture

No other book has impacted our team as much in the way that we worship. Understanding the ancient words of praise has given us a Biblical foundation to lead our church.

—**Jimi Williams**, Vice President, Creative, Capitol CMG Publishing

HOLY
ROAR

HOLY

THOMAS NELSON
Since 1798

ROAR

7 WORDS THAT WILL CHANGE
THE WAY YOU WORSHIP

CHRIS TOMLIN
AND
DARREN WHITEHEAD

Published in Nashville, Tennessee, by Thomas Nelson. Thomas Nelson is a registered trademark of HarperCollins Christian Publishing, Inc.

Copyright information for the songs discussed in this book can be found in the appendix.

Page design by Mandi Cofer

ISBN: 978-1-4002-1226-2

Printed in the United States of America

18 19 20 21 22 LSC 6 5 4 3 2 1

CONTENTS

About this Book   9

Introduction   12

One: The Hands of Praise   17

Two: The Fools of Praise   31

Three: The Music of Praise   43

Four: The Expectation of Praise   55

Five: The Posture of Praise   69

Six: The Songs of Praise   83

Seven: The Shout of Praise   95

Conclusion: The Practice of Praise   109

CONTENTS

Appendix   120

Notes   123

Acknowledgments   125

About the Authors   127

ABOUT THIS BOOK

It was Sunday morning in Franklin, Tennessee, and like so many in this small town, I was in church with my family. It was a Sunday on which I was not leading worship in another part of the country, a Sunday to rest with my own church family. So, this Sunday at Church of the City was already special. But what I didn't know as we sang the opening songs of praise was that this service would transform and deepen my understanding of praise and worship. It would change the way I led worship from that day forward.

That morning, my friend and pastor Darren Whitehead shared a message entitled "The Seven Words of Praise." It was a message that explained the different words the ancient Hebrew people used to express their praise to God. I was stirred by the depth of the expression of praise embodied by God's people. I kept thinking to myself, *I've been leading worship and writing songs for over twenty years. How have I never heard this before now?* This was a game changer for me.

Darren closed the sermon and said, "This will be your first time to experience worship with all this new knowledge." He smiled and held his hands out wide. "Make the most of it."

I was overcome as the music began to play, and if the response of the congregation was any indication, they were too. There was a palpable difference in the congregation's expression of worship after Darren's message, and it made the experience all the more overwhelming. A new sense of what it meant to praise God had taken hold; there was no turning back.

I may have waited an hour after the service before blowing up Darren's phone. I texted him, "Your message this morning was amazing. Everyone needs to know about the seven words of praise. It needs to be everywhere. Maybe even a book!"

It was the text message that would lead us to writing this book, *Holy Roar: 7 Words That Will Change the Way You Worship*.

This book is meant to deepen our collective understanding and experience of praise and worship. In each chapter, Darren helps us understand one of the Hebrew words for praise and invites us into that particular praise practice. After Darren's invitation, I'll share the story of a song I've written or recorded and how it relates to that particular word. We'll close each chapter with scriptures and reflection questions designed to lead you and your small group into a time of contemplation and discussion.

I am so excited you've picked up a copy of *Holy Roar*. I pray it becomes a resource to help you better understand just what it means when the scriptures say, "Praise the Lord!" I hope it will change the way you worship. I hope it will give you permission to join in the practices of praise, to become a part of the holy roar.

—Chris Tomlin

INTRODUCTION

I grew up in a rural town in South Australia, where I attended a small country church. The Christian tradition of my youth was not a particularly animated tribe. We were reserved, more conservative in the way we expressed ourselves in praise and worship. On any given Sunday, as we were led in traditional hymns (with a smattering of worship choruses), we'd sing along with sincere but subdued hearts. This is not to say, of course, that celebration wasn't happening in the pews, but the assumption was that any sort of celebration was personal, internal. As a general rule, implied though it was, expressions of outward, enthusiastic praise were not practiced.

Does this sound familiar? Did you come from a similar Christian tradition? If so, you can imagine my surprise when, at the invitation of a friend, I visited another sort of church. We'd arrived late, and the worship was in full swing when we walked in the back doors. This is what I saw: Some stood with a hand in the air; others raised two; some were squinting; one guy had a vein popping out of his neck; some were bouncing a little as they sang; one danced in the aisle and swung his hands. But no matter what their posture of praise was, everyone in the congregation was belting out the songs.

I can't say I really participated in the worship that day. Instead, I stood in the back, observing. By the end of the service, I had this distinct thought: *These are not my people.* And in a very real sense, I was uncomfortable with their outward displays of emotion and enthusiasm. Wasn't it all just a show? Even still, why was I strangely drawn to it? Why was I so curious? Tension was growing in my heart, a tension I'd not yet felt. And so, in that tension, I turned to my friend and said, "I'm very uncomfortable with all of this. See you next week!"

I went back to that church week after week, and after some time, I found myself unable to resist the passion of their praise. One day I couldn't hold back anymore, so I jumped into the river and sang with my whole heart. I poured myself out in that service, and though I didn't raise my hands or dance in the aisles, I became one of them.

Now, having pastored for around twenty years, I agree with the sentiments of the great Welsh theologian, Dr. Martyn Lloyd Jones, who argues that a dislike of enthusiasm can be "one of the greatest hindrances to revival."[1] Perhaps the secret to unlocking this sort of expressive enthusiasm might be found in a proper understanding of the seven Hebrew words of praise used in the Psalms.

If you've been in church for any length of time, you've heard there are four words that comprise the ancient Greek concept of love—*Storgē* (Στοργή), *Philia* (Φιλέω), *Eros* (Ερος), and *Agape* (Ἀγάπη). Though *Eros* (erotic love) doesn't appear in the New Testament text, whenever *Storgē* (natural love), *Philia* (brotherly love), and *Agape* (unconditional love) are used in the New Testament, each is translated simply as "love." In the language of the scriptures, you might *Storgē* sushi and *Agape* your child; in English, you love both. Using the same word for loving sushi and your children—doesn't that somehow diminish the word's impact?

Just as the New Testament translators did with the word *love*, Old Testament translators conflated seven primary Hebrew words into the single English word *praise*. Each of those words— *yâdâh*, *hâlal*, *zâmar*, *tôwdâh*, *bârak*, *tehillâh*, and *shâbach*—have distinct, important, and praise-altering implications. This book is my attempt to share the depth of meaning found in those seven Hebrew words.

Richard J. Foster said it best:

The Psalms are the literature of worship and their most prominent feature is praise. "Praise the Lord!" is the shout that reverberates from one end of the Psalter to the other. Singing, shouting, dancing, rejoicing, adoring—all are the language of praise.[2]

Are you ready to learn the full-bodied, expressive language of praise? Lean in as we explore the words for praise used in what Foster calls the literature of worship. Take notes. Understand the ways King David—the man after God's own heart—and the psalmists led the Hebrew people in praising God with their whole hearts and their whole bodies. As you do, see if you're not inspired to express your praise to God with a fresh enthusiasm. I think you will be.

Are you ready?

Let's jump in.

one

THE HANDS
OF PRAISE

יָדָה

YADAH

Yâdâh, yaw-daw´: To revere or worship with extended hands. To hold out the hands. To throw a stone or arrow.[3]

---

*May the peoples praise (yâdâh) you, God;
may all the peoples praise (yâdâh) you.*

—PSALM 67:3

t's true; in my youth, I was prone to poke fun at those who were expressive in worship. On a rare occasion, when someone dared to branch out with a raised hand in our otherwise stolid service, I'd lean over to one of my mates, or whoever might be sitting beside me, and I'd ask, "Do they need to go to the bathroom?" We'd get a good chuckle from the experience, then go back to singing our hymns, eyes fixed on the pages of those old hymnbooks. Hand-raisers, see, were outside the norms of our church subculture. They were too emotional, the folks on the edges.

As I wrote in the introduction, I followed my friend to a more expressive church in my early adulthood, and after a time, I became a regular attendee of that church. It was a church full of hand-raisers, kneelers, and dancers, and as much as I enjoyed their freedom to express their emotions in praise and worship, I clung to some of my more reserved tendencies: *Keep your eyes on the words. Don't get too emotional. Don't be a distraction.* Why didn't I feel the same freedom as the rest of the congregation? What was holding me back?

Freedom doesn't always come overnight, I suppose.

I wouldn't find the freedom to express myself in praise to God in a congregational setting—at least, not at first. Instead, God overcame my inhibitions in the privacy of my 1982 cherry-red Mazda RX-7. It was one of my first cars, one with a CD player and a distinct sense of *cool*. And cool as that car was, it surprised me when a friend gave me a CD to play while I drove around town, one that I prejudged as anything but *cool*.

The album was one of the first by Hillsong, and it was entitled *The Power of Your Love*. These were the days before the Hillsong craze, before they'd written so many of the songs sung in churches around the world. In fact, it was before the modern worship movement was in full swing. I'd never heard of Hillsong, so I asked what kind of music they played. It was a collection of worship songs and choruses, he said, and my response was less than pious.

"Church music? Why would I want to listen to that in my car?" I asked.

"Trust me, mate," he said. "You need to check this out."

He was a good friend, and I trusted him; so on his recommendation, I began listening to that CD. I listened and listened, and over the weeks that followed, something happened, something I didn't expect. I found myself in my car, not reaching for my old music—INXS, Midnight Oil, or Red Hot Chili Peppers. Instead, I began craving that early recording of Hillsong choruses. Those songs ambushed me, and as I listened, I found myself drawn into the presence of God. He was there, in that music, in my car, and it was in that expanding reality that I finally broke.

I was listening to *The Power of Your Love* on an afternoon just like any other. I pulled up to a stoplight, and in that moment, while waiting for the light to turn green, I was overcome by the goodness and power of God. Without a second thought, I took my hands from the steering wheel and lifted them. It was the most natural expression, and in that moment, I knew it: I'd become one of them. I'd switched teams.

I've been a hand-raiser ever since.

> Is there any more natural expression of excitement, wonder, or awe than raising your hands?

Is there any more natural expression of excitement, wonder, or awe than raising your hands? Whether it's the excitement that comes when your favorite sports team scores a goal, the joy of receiving an unexpected promotion, or the elation that comes with a declaration of victory in battle, aren't we prone to expressing enthusiasm with upshot hands? It's almost a primal instinct, something coded in our DNA. And regardless of the language you speak, the color of your skin, or your country of origin, haven't you felt this urge?

In the same way, the Hebrew people showed their excitement and enthusiasm for God in praise and worship by raising their hands. This posture of worship is expressed in the Psalms by the Hebrew word *yâdâh*.

Yâdâh is one of the seven words translated in the Old Testament as "praise," and it's found over 111 times in Scripture. It is defined as a word meaning to "extend hands" or "to throw out the hand," and it is used to describe the act of shooting an arrow (Jeremiah 50:14) or throwing a stone (Lamentations 3:53). In the context of praise, *yâdâh* describes those moments when the Hebrew people were so overcome by the glory of the Lord that their hands shot upward in response.

In Psalm 145:10, David wrote,

> All your works praise (*yâdâh*) you, LORD;
> your faithful people extol you.

In the psalm, David declares that God's people could not help but raise their hands in praise for God's faithfulness; they could not help but *yâdâh* the Lord.

In Psalm 67:3, the psalmist penned a song of praise for the people. The text reads,

> May the peoples praise (*yâdâh*) you, God;
> may all the peoples praise (*yâdâh*) you.

The psalm was certainly written for the Hebrew people, but doesn't the text imply a broader meaning? All the *peoples*, whether Hebrew or otherwise, raise their hands to God in praise. The people of Israel, the people of the early church, you, me—all of us who are part of the family of God will *yâdâh* our Father.

In Psalm 44:8, the psalmist wrote,

> In God we make our boast all day long,
> and we will praise (*yâdâh*) your name forever.

Yâdâh is not constrained to a particular time in history. Instead, the people of God will *yâdâh* for all eternity. Forever and ever. And though we've not yet reached the far shore of eternity, some three thousand years after this psalm was written, aren't God's people still praising him with raised hands?

One day, we will *yâdâh* our God forever and ever. Shouldn't we start practicing now?

Yâdâh—it's an active posture of praise expressed by those who adore God. It's an act of praise for all the people of God, whether charismatic, conservative, nondenominational, Baptist, Methodist, Catholic, or Presbyterian. What's more, it's an eternal verb, one that transcends time and place; and one day, we'll come to see that it transcends our own corporeal bodies too. One day, we will *yâdâh* our God forever and ever. Shouldn't we start practicing now?

BEHIND THE MUSIC
Holy Is the Lord

I was reared in a tradition of good, conservative, and Bible-believing folks who were buttoned up. We were not a people known for expressing emotion, especially in worship. So it should come as no surprise that I remember the scandalous moment a woman broke our house worship rules.

She was a middle-aged woman standing in a sea of four hundred congregants, and as the congregation moved into the chorus of some hymn we'd sung on hundreds of Sundays, she raised a single hand. It was an expression of adoration, of praise, but to the rest of the congregation it was alarming, a red flag, an indication of some sort of holy protest. The tension was palpable as a deacon crossed the sanctuary and asked her to lower her hand, to not make a scene, to conform.

We were not charismatic. We were not Holy Rollers. We were not people of raised hands.

Some years later, I attended a youth gathering where we sang songs with simpler melodies, songs of praise we called "choruses." Onstage, the leader led a song by the great worship pioneer, Dennis Jernigan. He built through the first verse, and as the chorus reached its crescendo, I felt the coming of a new freedom.

> And with our hands lifted high,
> we will worship and sing.
> And with our hands lifted high,
> we come before you rejoicing.
> With our hands lifted high to the sky,
> when the world wonders why.
> We'll just tell them we're loving our King.

Swept up in the chorus, I raised my hands for the first time, and in that simple act I began to understand—my expression of worship affected and reflected the posture of my heart toward God. In this simple act of lifting my hands, it felt as if I was lifting my heart, too, and it was the most natural act of praise.

Years passed, and I became a worship leader and songwriter in my own right. Following the lead of those like Jernigan, I made it a practice to incorporate postures of worship into my songs. Yet did I fully understand the power of the hand raised in praise?

In May 2003, I traveled to Sherman, Texas, for a worship

gathering called One Day, hosting over forty thousand university students. There, I saw this expression of praise come to life.

In the months before the One Day, I'd been working on a chorus—one I thought God had put on my heart specifically for this gathering. I lifted the chorus straight from the pages of Isaiah 6:3—"Holy is the LORD Almighty; the whole earth is full of his glory"—but I couldn't seem to find the right lyric for the verse. I approached my friend Louie Giglio, and he suggested I take a look at Nehemiah 8. "There's something there," he said. Following his lead, I opened the scriptures, and there, I found my missing lyrics. The verse flowed, almost without effort.

> We stand and lift up our hands
> for the joy of the Lord is our strength.
> We bow down and worship him, now.
> How great, how awesome is he!
> Together we sing,
> Holy is the Lord, God Almighty!
> The earth is full of his glory!

On that afternoon in May, I waited backstage to lead worship as notable preacher John Piper took the podium. If you know Dr. Piper, you know following him is no small task. Still unsure which song I'd lead after what was sure to be his incredible sermon, I listened for any cue. I was on my knees in the back-stage grass, asking God, "Please don't let me mess this up." John stood at that podium, surveying the crowd and letting the tension settle. A moment passed, and in his smooth baritone, he began.

"I have a word for you from Isaiah 6. 'Holy, holy, holy is the LORD Almighty; the whole earth is full of his glory.'"

I listened as he spoke of the majesty and glory of a holy God, and I knew it. God had given me the song "Holy Is the Lord" for this gathering, this day, these people. Dr. Piper finished his sermon, and I took the stage with the band. I looked over the crowd, this mass of forty thousand university students, knowing I was about to field-test a song. I strummed the opening chords and sang the first verse. I sang the verse and chorus, eyes closed in worship. When I circled back to the verse, I opened my eyes. That's when I noticed it: a wave of hands lifted in the sea of people. It was a collective act of praise, a natural expression of gratitude to a good and holy God.

One: The Hands of Praise
FOR REFLECTION AND DISCUSSION

But just as the lifting up of the hands is a symbol of confidence and longing, so in order to show our humility we fall down on our knees.
—JOHN CALVIN

Read the following verses:

Psalm 28:2

Psalm 63:4

Psalm 88:9

Psalm 134:2

Psalm 141:2

Psalm 143:6

Lamentations 3:41

1 Kings 8:22

Personal and group reflection questions:

1. Based on the above verses, how common do you think the practice of lifting hands in worship was in the ancient world?

2. Do you regularly praise God by lifting your hands? If so, think about or describe the first time you remember lifting your hands in worship in a public setting.

3. Read the quote by John Calvin. Do any words or phrases stand out to you? How do these words impact the way you think about praising God?

4. How do you think lifting hands represents confidence and longing?

5. What are we communicating to God when we lift our hands?

two

THE FOOLS
OF PRAISE

הָלַל

HALAL

Hâlal, haw-lal´: To boast. To rave. To shine. To celebrate. To be clamorously foolish.[4]

Let them praise (hâlal) his name with dancing and make music to him with timbrel and harp.

—PSALM 149:3

A couple of years ago my wife and I were invited to a Jewish wedding. I'd never been to one before and had no idea what I was getting into. There were differences in the ceremony—that much is true—but the culmination of the wedding was just like any other. There were vows, a kiss, and a pronouncement. There was a new union—husband and wife.

After the ceremony, we made our way to the reception where the real fun and games began. A huge banquet awaited us—a spread of food and drinks as impressive as any I'd ever seen at a wedding. There was grand music and dancing, and everyone shouted and laughed in celebration. And though I was the Gentile of Gentiles in the room (how else would you describe a Christian preacher at a Jewish wedding?), I quickly found that participation in this party was not optional.

I was watching the rowdy festivities when, without warning, two yarmulke-wearing men in their mid-sixties sandwiched me between them. Seconds later, I was swept into a dance with these two strangers, and after a few moments, as if on cue, both men threw their heads back and laughed with such energy that it seemed to come from their very souls. These guys knew how to have fun, but even more importantly, they knew how to draw others into their party. They knew that the cosmic union of souls, the coming together of two people in holy matrimony, was a thing worthy of foolish, near-nonsensical celebration. The celebration was for everyone, Jew and Gentile alike.

The wedding was an amazing experience, and those men personified a word I'd read in the Hebrew text of the Old Testament. It was a word of praise, a word used again and again throughout the book of Psalms—*hâlal*.

Hâlal is the primary Hebrew word for praise. It's the word from which we derive the biblical word *hallelujah*. It's an exuberant expression of celebration, a word that connotes boasting, raving, or celebrating. It carries with it the notion of acting in a way that is "clamorously foolish." True *hâlal* contemplates laying aside your inhibitions and killing your self-consciousness.

It's an exuberant expression of celebration, a word that connotes boasting, raving, or celebrating.

In the Old Testament, the word *hilul* (which comes from the same root word) is used in two places outside the psalms. In both the book of Judges and the book of Leviticus, it is used to describe the way the people might celebrate a harvest festival. There, they'd dance on the grapes, expressing the harvest's juices for use in wine making. Imagine their enthusiasm as they danced and danced, as the hems of their robes were dyed purple. This dance carries with it the idea of *hâlal.*

Hâlal is used throughout the psalms. Psalm 69:30 reads, "I will praise (*hâlal*) God's name in song." Psalm 22:22 reads, "I will declare your name to my people; in the assembly I will praise (*hâlal*) you." In Psalm 109:30, the psalmist wrote, "With my mouth I will greatly extol the LORD; in the great throng of worshippers I will praise (*hâlal*) him." But though these psalms were written in the first person, they were often sung corporately.

Because psalms of *hâlal* were not static declarations, because they were meant for corporate celebration, let's consider the shape of that celebration using Psalm 149:3. The text of the psalm is simple:

Let them praise (*hâlal*) his name with dancing
and make music to him with timbrel and harp.

Imagine the Hebrew people gathered together. There, tens of thousands of Levites and musicians faced the Israelites, and together, they formed a sort of praise pit. The Levites and musicians played, and as their songs rose, a combustible energy built and built and built until some spark of God ignited the praises of the people. In that moment, the worshippers began to shout, laugh, and dance. They jumped around, hands raised. To the outside observer, they might have appeared drunk or foolish, but they were most sober in their celebration of God; they were incarnating *hâlal*.

The concept of *hâlal* is so embedded in the notion of praise that it serves as a capstone to the entire book of Psalms. In Psalm 150:6, the writer concludes, "Let everything that has breath praise (*hâlal*) the LORD."

The God of the universe made us to praise him with abandon, like foolish but fun-loving children. Sometimes I wonder if God looks down on North America, if he sees our dignified, carefully orchestrated worship experiences, and wishes we'd cut loose. I wonder if he wishes we'd celebrate him the way those two Jewish gentlemen celebrated at that wedding I attended. I wonder if he wishes we'd join the party, that we'd step out onto his great dance floor and risk being undignified.

God is inviting us into *hâlal*. Will you let go? Will you enter his courts with dancing?

BEHIND THE MUSIC
God's Great Dance Floor

There are songs that seem to come from nowhere, that take me by surprise, and "God's Great Dance Floor" was one of those songs.

In early 2012, Martin Smith and I met for a writing session. He'd written an extended ballad entitled "Back to the Start," which explored prodigal themes of return and rescue. He played me a demo of the song, haunting as it was.

> Back to the start where you found me,
> I give you my heart again.
> Take everything; I'm all I can bring,
> I'm coming home again.

It was a beautiful song—melodic, almost transfixing. And just when I thought the song might end, it began to build, and build, and build into a closing refrain of celebration: "I feel alive on God's great dance floor."

"What was that?" I asked, taken by the ending of the song.

"It's the prodigal return," he said. "When we come back to the father, he throws a party. It's not a time of lament, but a time for celebration, to dance like a child."

I said I loved it, and I asked whether we could rip the ending and form it into its own song. Martin laughed, and in his thick English accent, said, "Mate, there are no rules. We can do what we want."

Months after we ripped the ending into its own song, I found myself at Passion 2013 in Atlanta, Georgia. I had an idea:

We'd find a mariachi trumpeter to play with us when we led the song for the first time at the conference. And so, before the event, I found a trumpeter at a local Mexican restaurant while he was playing with his band. I knew he'd be perfect.

At the conference, we prepared to take the stage, and the mariachi trumpeter stood by in full regalia. He held his trumpet by his side, relaxed, not quite aware of the magnitude of the moment. My bandmates looked at him, looked at me, then looked at him again.

"It's not too late to call it off," one said.

Worship—so often it's more about the seeing than the singing. Those sorts of celebrations might be a little rowdy, a little raucous, a little undignified, even. But isn't this the essence of *hâlal*?

I shook my head. "Trust me. Something will shake loose when he takes the stage. That crowd will see the truth—that this is a party."

And shake loose it did.

We cycled through the verse and chorus of "God's Great Dance Floor," and just before the instrumental break, the trumpeter walked onto the stage. The crowd kept clapping, kept moving, but you could see it; they were transfixed by this man who seemed so out of place in the moment. He raised his trumpet, and when he played the first note, the stadium erupted. It was a dance party, a party of praise. It was a party fit for the return of the prodigals, the return of all those sons and daughters.

The band and I have talked about that moment over these last few years. That song, the mariachi player, all of it served to let the worshippers *see* the sort of celebration our Father throws in our prodigal return. (Worship—so often it's more about the seeing than the singing.) Those sorts of celebrations might be a little rowdy, a little raucous, a little undignified, even. But isn't this the essence of *hâlal*?

Two: The Fools of Praise
FOR REFLECTION AND DISCUSSION

The most valuable thing the psalms do for me is to express the same delight in God which made David dance.

—C.S. LEWIS

Read the following verses:

Psalm 150
Luke 15:23–24
Ecclesiastes 3:4
Philippians 4:4
Psalm 30:11
Acts 3:8

Personal and group reflection questions:

1. Based on these verses, what words would you use to describe praising God?

2. If you grew up attending church, think about or describe a typical church service. Was it an outwardly expressive, enthusiastic environment of praising God?

3. Read the quote by C.S. Lewis. Do any words or phrases stand out to you? How do these words impact the way you think about praising God?

4. Why do you think some people are hesitant to express their celebration in a church gathering?

5. When you praise God in a public setting, how conscious are you of others around you?

three

THE MUSIC
OF PRAISE

זָמַר

ZAMAR

Zâmar, zaw-mar´: To make music. To celebrate in song and music. To touch the strings or parts of a musical instrument.[5]

I will sing a new song to You, O God;
On a harp of ten strings I will sing praises (zâmar) to You.
—PSALM 144:9 NKJV

stood over Brandy, looking into her eyes, giving her chips of ice, holding her hand, doing whatever she needed. She was deep into labor with our third daughter, Violet, and as was the tradition in the Whitehead family, music filled the hospital room.

In the weeks before delivery, Brandy and I made a worship playlist. We'd done the same thing when our first two daughters were born. More than anything, we wanted the songs of the church to be the first sounds our daughters' tiny ears ever heard; we wanted to bring them into the chorus of God's family from the beginning.

The worship music we played during Brandy's labor gave us a sort of hidden strength. This music wasn't just for our new baby. It was for us too. The people of God singing the praises of God calmed us through the moments of anxiety, bolstering Brandy's spirits even through the labor of childbirth. The music was a conduit of God's grace, and we felt it in that hospital room.

Praise and worship music can be a powerful tool to draw us into a personal experience with God. And this effect can be felt in the privacy of a hospital room or in the gathering of the church. Haven't you experienced this? Consider that time you walked into church, frustrated with a friend, anxious about your finances, perhaps concerned about a new health challenge. Remember how you stood in the liminal space before the worship music began and made small talk as best you could, the things of eternity far from your mind. Recall how the chords began to fill the room, how the attention of the crowd was turned toward the praise of God. In that moment, didn't the stuff of earth, the anxieties of life, seem to melt into the melody? As the cares rolled away, didn't you encounter the very presence of God?

Music is more powerful than we even understand. It can soften our hearts, soothe our troubled souls. It opens a door to the spiritual world. It paves the road for the Spirit's coming.

Music is more powerful than we even understand. It can soften our hearts, soothe our troubled souls. It opens a door to the spiritual world. It paves the road for the Spirit's coming. The patriarchs, psalmists, and prophets of the scriptures understood the power of music especially. Recall the story of Elisha.

In the book of 2 Kings, we see the sons of Israel, poised on the edge of battle with Moab, and their water stores had run dry. Some of the men wondered aloud whether there might be a prophet in their ranks, someone who could consult with God on their behalf. In that moment, Elisha stepped forward, saying he had come bearing the word of the Lord. Before he would speak the prophecy, though, he demanded a soundtrack. "Bring me a harpist," he said, then waited. And when the harpist came, when the music finally played, Elijah stood and delivered the Word of God, saying: "This is what the LORD says: I will fill this valley with pools of water" (2 Kings 3:15–16).

Elisha knew the power of a good soundtrack, how it frames a moment. Music so often prepares the heart for the reality of an important message. This reality is captured by the third Hebrew word that's so often translated as praise—the word *zâmar*.

Zâmar is used throughout the psalms to connote the making of music, celebrating in song and music, and plucking the strings of a musical instrument. It's a word that appears in the scriptures forty-one times, both in narrative form and in the poetry of the psalms.

In Psalm 144:9 (NKJV), the psalmist wrote:

I will sing a new song to You, O God;
On a harp of ten strings I will sing praises (*zâmar*) to You.

In Psalm 7:17 (NKJV), the writer incorporated the idea of raising hands of praise to music of praise, writing:

> I will praise (*yâdâh*) the Lord according to His righteousness,
> And will sing praise (*zâmar*) to the name of the Lord
> Most High.

Some believed David wrote Psalm 57 while he was hiding from King Saul in a desert cave. In it, he wrote:

> My heart is fixed, O God,
> my heart is fixed:
> I will sing and give praise (*zâmar*).
> (Psalm 57:7 KJV)

David recognized the truth Elisha understood. Music can bolster the human heart, can fill us with the courage to exercise our faith as we live into the promises of God.

It's easy to read the psalms as personal expressions of praise and worship, as written by and for a particular writer. But as we've already seen, so many of these psalms were sung corporately by the people of God, and when the songs were raised together, they were almost always accompanied by instrumentation. Why? The psalmists understood the role of music in penetrating the hearts of people. They understood how our hearts reverberate in tune with instruments played for God.

We're not all able to play the piano or guitar. We can't all pluck the strings of a musical instrument, and some of us can't carry a tune in a bucket. But that doesn't mean we can't engage in *zâmar*. As we listen to music, can't we recognize the way it prepares our souls to receive God's Word? Can't we allow it to soften us? Can't we appreciate how it serves as a vehicle, carrying our praise to the throne of God? When we do, we're participating in *zâmar*.

If you are a musician, ask yourself: *When is the last time I simply played my instrument for God alone? When is the last time I felt the power of God in my music, even when no words were sung?* Making music, *zâmar*, is a gift. Are you making the most of it?

BEHIND THE MUSIC
Instrumental Praise

In the earliest days of leading worship, I read the story of the famous composer, Johann Sebastian Bach. It's said that as Bach composed and played music, it was as if he were praising God, even in his instrumental arrangements. "I play the notes as they are written," Bach is oft quoted as saying, "but it is God who makes the music." Bach was so convinced of this truth, in fact, that he penned the initials S.D.G. on many of his pieces, his shorthand for *Soli Deo gloria*—glory to God alone.

Bach's commitment to creating music to the glory of God was inspirational and formative, and it put language to my practice of prayer before leading worship. Even before reading about Bach's commitment, I'd prayed that God would be in the music that I played, that I'd simply reflect the melodies God put on my heart, whether or not those songs included words.

There's something about those times of instrumental worship, times when we *pluck the string*. They've been some of the most powerful times of personal worship for me. And though it's hard to explain, they are the times I've most felt that I was playing the soundtrack of God.

Over the years, I've had the privilege to play with some of the most incredible musicians, people truly gifted to lead the church in worship. There are times, though, when we gather for the purpose of simply playing. We'll come together to play impromptu instrumental pieces without singing a word. In these moments, rare though they may be, we try our best to pay attention to each other, to the rhythms, to the melodies, and to the harmonies God puts on our hearts. As best as we can, we try to play those songs to the glory of God alone.

There's something about those times of instrumental worship, times when we *pluck the string*. They've been some of the most powerful times of personal worship for me. And though it's hard to explain, they are the times I've most felt that I was playing the soundtrack of God. In such times I felt Bach's truth most.

Yes, I play the notes as they come, but God makes the music. I'm his instrument, a reflection of his music, and before I step onto any stage, I ask that the touch of his presence would be on the music I play. I ask that no matter the crowd size, no matter the songs we play, no matter the time of day, may we play every song for the glory of God alone. Isn't this the greatest privilege?

FOR REFLECTION AND DISCUSSION

Next to the Word of God, the noble art of music is the greatest treasure in the world. Beautiful music is the art of the prophets that can calm the agitations of the soul; it is one of the most magnificent and delightful presents God has given us.

—MARTIN LUTHER

Read the following verses:

Ephesians 5:19

Colossians 3:16

Psalm 33:1–4

1 Samuel 16:23

Psalm 150:4

Psalm 144:9

Psalm 101:1

Personal and group reflection questions:

1. Based on these verses, how common do you think the practice of music was in the ancient world?

2. Do you play a musical instrument? If so, how does playing music help you to express your heart of praising God?

3. Read the quote by Martin Luther. Do any words or phrases stand out to you? How do these words impact the way you think about praising God?

4. What role has music played in your spiritual journey?

5. How does music impact your heart, thoughts, and emotions?

four

THE
EXPECTATION
OF PRAISE

תּוֹדָה

TOWDAH

Tôwdâh, to-daw´: An extension of the hand.
Thanksgiving. A confession. A sacrifice of praise.
Thanksgiving for things not yet received. A choir
of worshippers.[6]

In God I have put my trust;
I will not be afraid.
What can man do to me?
Vows made to You are binding upon me, O God;
I will render praises (tôwdâh) to You.

—PSALM 56:11–12 NKJV

A few years ago, I was invited to speak at Salem Baptist Church, the largest African-American church in Chicagoland. The church boasts twenty thousand members and is pastored by Reverend James Meeks. They meet in Chicago's South Side, an area with a high concentration of crime. It's an area known for its violence and gangs, and shootings taking place in the neighborhoods around the church often make their way into national headlines.

I was nervous about visiting Salem Baptist Church. First, I'd never preached at a predominately black church. Perhaps more daunting, though, was the task of preaching in a community surrounded by such spiritual resistance. I thought the church must feel that resistance, that they must be weighed down by all the violence. I wondered if the tension would be palpable.

I sat on the front row on the Sunday morning I was scheduled to preach, and I waited for the service to begin. The choir filed in, and even before they took the stage, they began belting out their song.

"The Lord made a way when there was no way," they sang.

> "Rise up, church!"
> "God is not done yet."
> "My Deliverer is coming."

They continued to their places, singing over the church, asking them to rise up in song with them.

Tôwdâh is a Hebrew word that means an extension of the hand in thanksgiving for what God has done. But it also means a sacrifice of praise for things not yet received. It is praising God with expectation.

The choir continued lifting praise for what seemed like an hour. They declared that their story, the story of the community, was not over yet, that they would rise up and stand in faith. They declared that they would hold to that faith, the faith that the Lord would come through. They sang for things they hadn't yet experienced, the coming of peace and perfect freedom. They didn't hold back. It was, maybe, the most stirring worship experience I'd ever had, and as I listened to those songs I was overtaken. I began to sing with them; and as if swept into the current of their praise, I sensed the outpouring of fresh faith filling the room, filling me.

It came time for me to preach, and I didn't walk to the pulpit; I floated up to it. There was something about this congregation's declaration of faith. I sensed their strength. Despite all the darkness in their community, all the violence and gang activity, they would not back down. They rejoiced in the light of God, holding to his promises in expectation that he would move. In that expectation, God saw fit to pour out his blessing, his presence. He inhabited that room.

This was my most vivid recollection of experiencing the power of expectant praise. This was an experience of *tôwdâh*.

Tôwdâh is a Hebrew word that means an extension of the hand in thanksgiving for what God has done. But it also means a sacrifice of praise for things not yet received. It is praising God with expectation. The psalmist used *tôwdâh* as an expression of confession, a way to convey trust in the goodness of God.

It was a word of thanksgiving, a word often raised by choirs of worshippers.

In Psalm 50, the psalmist Asaph recorded a stanza for the wicked, for those who'd forgotten their God. The stanza culminated with a promise for those who practiced *tôwdâh*:

> Now consider this, you who forget God,
> Lest I tear you in pieces,
> And there be none to deliver:

> Whoever offers praise (*tôwdâh*) glorifies Me;
> And to him who orders his conduct aright
> I will show the salvation of God.
> (Psalm 50:22–23 NKJV)

Asaph's psalm makes it plain: Sometimes the sacrifice of praise, the act of showing God honor and praise even before the realization of his promises, precedes salvation.

In most Bibles, Psalm 56 is preceded by a notation indicating it was written by David after he was seized by the Philistines at Gath. Despite his capture, despite the direst of circumstances, David wrote:

> In God I have put my trust;
> I will not be afraid.
> What can man do to me?
> Vows made to You are binding upon me, O God;
> I will render praises (*tôwdâh*) to You.
> (Psalm 56:11–12 NKJV)

David, captured by the enemy and facing an unknown future, praised the Lord for the promise of deliverance he'd not yet received. He knew he'd be delivered, so in his imprisonment, he praised God in earnest expectation.

In *tôwdâh*, we lift our hands in the presence of God, not only for what he has done, but also for what we believe he will do. He will bring an end to all violence, so we lift our hands in praise. He will release us from bondage, so we lift our hands in praise. He will provide what we need, so we lift our hands in praise. He will heal us, both now and in eternity, so we lift our hands in praise.

The notion of lifting hands in praise to God as a sign of faith for promises to come is most biblical. And when we engage in this expression, when we raise our hands heavenward, we're pointing to the very place of our ultimate hope. As David said in Psalm 20:7,

> Some trust in chariots and some in horses,
> but we trust in the name of the LORD our God.

I once knew a man, Ken, who had a way of pointing to the place of ultimate hope, even in times of deep anxiety. One day he called me into his office and told me his teenage daughter had been out partying. She had not come home, and no one could find her. As he told me the story, I interrupted and said, "You must be worried out of your mind." His answer was quick and calm.

"I don't worry. I worship."

I've never forgotten those words. Instead of focusing on the things out of his control, he turned his attention to the One who is in control. He worshipped God, believing he'd respond. He moved his worry to worship. I've thought about Ken many times over the years in seasons of stress and anxiety. Ken was practicing the essence of *tôwdâh*.

Have you raised your hands in praise, believing in faith that God will fulfill his promises to you? Have you raised your hands for your wounded marriage, your troubled career, your wayward son or daughter? Have you raised your hands believing God will give you the guidance and the direction you so desperately need? Have you raised *tôwdâh* to God for healing?

Our praise should embody the notion of *tôwdâh*; it should become an expression of faith for salvation not yet received. My friends at Salem Baptist Church in Chicago know this full well. Would you let their story of *tôwdâh* wash over you and lead you into a fuller expression of praise?

BEHIND THE MUSIC
I Lift My Hands

It was 2009, and my dear friend Louie was struggling. We'd been in ministry together for years by then, and I'd watched him lead thousands of college students into a deeper relationship with God. I'd seen God spark movements of the Spirit on every continent through Louie. He'd founded Passion City Church, the church where I led worship. He was successful. Accomplished. He was solid. He was the last person I expected to sink into a dark night.

My friend was experiencing what so many have experienced, what so many experience even today. Louie was battling anxiety.

He'd been to the doctors, had test after test run. No good answers came. He could manage in the day, he said, but every night, around two o'clock in the morning, the anxious thoughts came rushing in.

One afternoon Louie began to tell me about a song he'd been singing in that two o'clock hour. He would sing this song over and over to himself in defiance of the darkness. I asked him if I could hear it, but he said, "The melody is probably pretty terrible, so let me just tell you the words."

> Be still, my soul, there is a healer.
> His love is deeper than the sea.
> His mercy is unfailing.
> His arms a fortress for the weak.
> I lift my hands to believe again.

Days later, my friend Matt Maher and I met, and we began to write a melody around Louie's midnight lyrics. Those words of Louie's were his song, a holy song, so we didn't change a word. Considering a chorus, I turned to the psalms and found my way to Psalm 42:4, where David wrote, "These things I remember as I pour out my soul: how I used to go to the house of God under the protection of the Mighty One with shouts of joy and praise among the festive throng."

When I feel the dark times setting in, the pains of life, I sing this song and lift my hands in expectation that the darkness will not live.

Matt and I played the verse, built into the chorus, and words came pouring out.

> I lift my hands to believe again.
> You are my refuge, you are my strength.
> As I pour out my heart these things I remember,
> You are faithful God forever.
> Let faith arise. Let faith arise.

64

The weeks wore on, and though Louie began to feel some relief, he didn't immediately experience complete healing. In those weeks, I introduced "I Lift My Hands" at Passion City Church, the song that incorporated Louie's midnight words. On rare occasions, a song takes hold of a congregation and immediately becomes part of its fabric. This was that kind of song. Over the following weeks, as we sang, I could see it providing all of us with newfound strength.

"I Lift My Hands" has become an anthem for more than me, more than Louie, and more than any one church. It's become a song for many who find themselves in dark seasons. It's a song of expectation. When I feel the dark times setting in, the pains of life, I sing this song and lift my hands in expectation that the darkness will not live. God will lead me into the land of the living. He is faithful forever.

Let faith arise.

Four: The Expectation of Praise
FOR REFLECTION AND DISCUSSION

*True worship that is pleasing to God
creates within the human heart a spirit of
expectation and insatiable longing.*
—A.W. TOZER

Read the following verses:

Psalm 141:2

Psalm 88:9

Hebrews 11:6

1 Corinthians 2:5

Habakkuk 3:2

2 Corinthians 5:7

Psalm 121:1–2

Psalm 20:7

Personal and group reflection questions:

1. After reading these verses, what impact do you think
   praising God has on your personal faith in him?

2. Think about or describe a time when you have seen God answer a specific prayer or specific need that you had.

3. Read the quote by A.W. Tozer. Do any words or phrases stand out to you? How do these words impact the way you think about praising God?

4. How is your faith impacted when you are among other believers when they are praising God?

5. Is there something that you are currently asking God for? Have you offered praise (*tôwdâh*) in faith that he would answer you?

five

THE POSTURE
OF PRAISE

בָּרַךְ

BARAK

Bârak, baw-rak´: To kneel. To bless God (as an act of adoration). To praise. To salute. To thank.[7]

Yea, all kings shall fall down before him: all nations shall serve him . . .

And he shall live, and to him shall be given of the gold of Sheba: prayer also shall be made for him continually; and daily shall he be praised (bârak).

—PSALM 72:11, 15 KJV

Years ago, I received a phone call while driving to church. It was from an unknown number, and the voice on the other side of the line told me Rickey, a student from my days of youth pastoring, had been in a serious motorcycle accident in Franklin. He was in a coma, the voice said, and had been life-flighted to Vanderbilt Hospital. I was living in Chicago at the time, but Rickey was one of those special kids, one for whom I had deep affection. So I dropped everything and made my way to Nashville.

After a whirlwind flight, I made my way to the hospital. There, I saw Rickey lying in his bed, near lifeless. He'd been married the year before, and his wife was in the room, desperate. The doctors had told us that it would be critical to see some improvement in Rickey's condition in the first twenty-four hours, so we made his hospital room a place of prayer. We begged. We pleaded. We cried out to God.

Despite our prayers, no change occurred. A day passed, then another. A third day, a fourth day, a fifth. Just before I was scheduled to return to Chicago, a doctor came, telling us that the chances of his survival were incredibly remote, and that with every passing moment, the likelihood of his death increased exponentially.

The doctor left the room, and a nurse came in. She looked at Rickey's wife and said, "In situations like this, hard decisions need to be made. Sometimes it helps to talk those decisions out. I've been sent to have that conversation with you." Rickey's wife collapsed on the spot, sobbing uncontrollably.

When it came time for me to leave, Rickey's wife hadn't yet made any decisions. I hugged her, gathered my things, and made my way back to Chicago. I was not hopeful.

The next Sunday, back in Chicago, I was driving to church and talking on the phone with my best mate of more than twenty years, Jon Tyson. Jon, also a pastor, had virtually raised Rickey after his dad had died when he was young. With devastated hearts, we started discussing the logistics of the impending funeral service. We talked about who would officiate it. Jon said, "I don't know if I could get through it. He was like a son to me." We sat with the weight of that statement for a few seconds until he broke the silence.

"Hold on. I'm getting another call."

While he tended to business on his other line, I waited, heavyhearted. How could this thing happen to Rickey? How could I worship God in the heaviness of everything?

After a few moments, the phone silence was broken by Jon's voice. "Rickey just woke up," he said, and we both burst into tears.

I walked into the church, through the lobby, and into the main auditorium. There, Brandy and I entered with such gratitude, such praise. And as the music began, I looked at Brandy, now on her knees, arms outstretched, thanking God for the miracle he'd done. In that moment, I joined her, and together we wept in joy as we fixed our eyes on the Giver of life.

> *Bârak* embodies the notion of kneeling before God, of blessing and adoring him, of recognizing one's position in relation to him.

For the rest of my life, whenever I read Psalm 100, I will think of that moment.

Psalm 100:4 says,

> Enter his gates with thanksgiving
> and his courts with praise (*tehillâh*);
> give thanks to him and praise (*bârak*) his name.

It's a psalm of praise springing from thanksgiving. It's the idea of falling to your knees in adoration and gratitude.

The fifth word commonly translated as praise, the word *bârak*, is a word of humility. *Bârak* embodies the notion of kneeling before God, of blessing and adoring him, of recognizing one's position in relation to him. It's a word used 289 times in the psalms, and on each occurrence, it's used to describe worshippers falling on their faces before God in reverence, adoration, and thanks.

Scholars of the ancient Hebrew provide additional insights into the word *bârak*. They believe that in the original context, the term did not simply mean bowing down. Instead, it carried the connotation of bending low while keeping one's eyes fixed on the king. To *bârak* is to be transfixed.

Psalm 72, a psalm of Solomon, uses *bârak* to describe the ways the kings of the nations bow to the one true King. Solomon wrote it this way:

> Yea, all kings shall fall down before him:
> all nations shall serve him . . .
> And he shall live,
> and to him shall be given of the gold of Sheba:
> prayer also shall be made for him continually;
> and daily shall he be praised (*bârak*).
> (Psalm 72:11, 15 KJV)

In *bârak*, even the most powerful lay aside their egos, their power, their desires. They offer all they have—their gold, their prayer, their honor, their gaze.

In Psalm 103, David used the phrase *bârak* as a repetitive hook, writing,

> Praise (*bârak*) the LORD, my soul;
> all my inmost being, praise his holy name.
> Praise (*bârak*) the LORD, my soul,
> and forget not all his benefits . . .
> Praise (*bârak*) the LORD, you his angels,
> you mighty ones who do his bidding,
> who obey his word.
> Praise (*bârak*) the LORD, all his heavenly hosts,
> you his servants who do his will.
> Praise (*bârak*) the LORD, all his works
> everywhere in his dominion.
> Praise (*bârak*) the LORD, my soul.
> (Psalm 103:1–2, 20–22)

In Psalm 103, all things are commanded to *bârak* the Lord. The angels and mighty ones, the saints who've gone before us, the works of the Lord, his creation, even our very souls, tethered to these temporary bodies—David commands all of it to *bârak* the true King.

I often wonder how our church gatherings might feel if, Sunday after Sunday, we came with the eyes of our souls transfixed on the King. Would we complain about the music, about the song selection, about the volume? If we were bowed down, eyes on the King, would we care?

At Church of the City, we've done our best to incorporate the notion of *bârak*, of keeping our eyes turned to Jesus in worship. When debriefing a church service over lunch, often we ask the question, "How was the worship?" We encourage people to respond with "That's the wrong question!" The better questions are "How was your worship?" and "How was my worship?" It's a question of self-examination, a reminder that when we come into the presence of God together, our sole focus should be on the King.

If we've experienced the goodness of God, if we've seen him at work in our lives, in the lives of our friends, in the life of our church, how can we not *bârak*? How can we not fall to our knees in gratitude with our eyes fixed on him?

BEHIND THE MUSIC
We Fall Down

It was the late 1990s, a time when the modern praise and worship movement was just taking hold. I'd traveled throughout college leading worship for youth retreats and church camps, and the summer after my senior year, I'd booked twelve camps in twelve weeks. One of those camps featured a dynamic young speaker from Atlanta.

These were the days before Louie and I were close friends, before our ministries had become so intertwined, and as I listened to him preach night after night, I was taken by the way he brought the scriptures to life. Midway through the camp, he asked the students to turn to Revelation 4, and as he read the scriptures, he brought us to the throne room of God. He showed us Christ, seated at the right hand of God, showed how people of every tongue, tribe, and nation came before that throne and presented their crowns, their accomplishments, to the King of the universe. And this, he said, wasn't just some event that would happen in the future. This casting down of crowns happened day by day, hour by hour, minute by minute. It was a present reality. One day, he said, it would be our turn to cast down our crowns.

After my closing worship set, I returned to my dorm room, still considering that reality. There, I returned to Revelation 4, where the apostle John wrote,

Day and night they never stop saying:

> "'Holy, holy, holy
> Is the Lord God Almighty,'
> who was, and is, and is to come" . . .

Elders fall down before him who sits on the throne and worship him who lives for ever and ever. They lay their crowns before the throne and say:

"You are worthy, our Lord and God."
(vv. 8, 10–11)

As I contemplated the beauty and humility of the scriptures, the bowing down of the worshippers, I began to play a simple melody, singing, "We fall down; we lay our crowns at the feet of Jesus." It was a musical representation of a spiritual reality. It was my attempt to lay my own crowns down, even in that moment.

In the early hours of the morning, I finished the song "We Fall Down." Excited, a bit nervous, and young enough to not be bothered by social norms, I grabbed my guitar and made my way to Louie's dorm. I knocked on his door, and he answered, sleepy-eyed.

"I just wrote this song from the message you preached tonight," I said, "and I'd like to play it for you."

He leaned against his door. "Now?" he asked.

"Yeah. Now."

In his dorm room, I sat on the side of his bed and sang my recasting of Revelation 4. He stared at the floor, rocking as I sang, and when I finished, he let the silence linger. After a moment's pause, he looked up and stared at me for an uncomfortable moment.

"Chris, I think the whole world is going to sing that song."

"Well, I was just hoping we could sing it tomorrow at camp. I don't know anything about the whole world."

I played the song the next day. In fact, I played it the next week, and the week after that. As I traveled from camp to camp, the song seemed to take on a life of its own. It became the first song I published, the first of my songs sung in churches in any significant way. In the years following, I discovered that "We Fall Down" had been translated into Spanish, Setswana, American Sign Language, and many other languages. It was a song of global praise, a song in which people from all walks declared their need to get low before God, to bow in the glory of his presence, eyes fixed on him.

FOR REFLECTION AND DISCUSSION

Fall on your knees
O hear the angel voices
O night divine
O night when Christ was born
O night divine
O night divine.

—FROM "O HOLY NIGHT" BY PLACIDE CAPPEAU (1847)

Read the following verses:

Psalm 95:6

Ezekiel 3:23

Ephesians 3:14

Daniel 6:10

Ezra 9:5

Romans 14:11

Acts 20:36

Revelation 7:11

Personal and group reflection questions:

1. Based on these verses, how common do you think the worship practice of kneeling down was in the ancient world?

2. The root meaning for the Hebrew word we translate worship is "to prostrate." The word *bless* literally means "to kneel." Can you think of a time when you had a meaningful experience kneeling before the Lord?

3. Read the lyrics from "O Holy Night" by Placide Cappeau. Do any words or phrases stand out to you? How do these words impact the way you think about praising God?

4. What does kneeling before God communicate to him?

5. How often do you take time to kneel before God? Is this something you wish to do more?

six

THE SONGS
OF PRAISE

תְּהִלָּה

TEHILLAH

Tehillâh, teh-hil-law´: Laudation. A hymn. A song of praise. A new song. A spontaneous song.[8]

But You are holy,
Enthroned in the praises (tehillâh) of Israel.
—PSALM 22:3 NKJV

Almost twenty years ago, I applied for a work visa to enter the United States. I was working at a Christian radio station in Adelaide at the time, yet I felt an unusual sense of calling to move to America. After several hours on the phone with officers from the US Consulate office in Melbourne, I learned that I did not qualify for a US work visa. Despite that information, I decided to apply anyway, then packed all my earthly possessions into two bags and flew to Melbourne.

With a whole host of other Australians, I took my place in line at the US Consulate office in downtown Melbourne. After answering a few questions and enduring a short wait, I was given my visa for entry into the United States, but after giving it a once-over, I realized they'd made a mistake. I'd been issued a pastor's visa, a religious worker's visa.

A pastor's visa?

I'd never been to seminary. I didn't plan on going to seminary. I'd never been a pastor. I didn't plan on being a pastor. Sure, I worked in Christian radio, but it was more than a stretch to call me a bona fide minister. Visa in hand, though, I made my way to the States, and when I arrived I found a fantastic church. Before long I joined the staff of that church. Sometimes people ask me, "How do you know you were called to be a pastor?" I respond, "The US government called me into this!" Then I add, "And out of fear of deportation, I just keep preaching every week!"

This is my story—the story of how I ended up as an accidental preacher in America. It's a song that has not been put to music yet, but I'd submit that if Chris did it, it would be a worship hit among Australian green card holders!

How many songs have grown from a writer's personal experience? As you've read this book, as you've read the stories behind Chris's music, you've seen that his songs are nothing if not storied praise. And in this way, Chris's music stands in the great traditions of the psalms. The Old Testament psalmists were masters incorporating their stories into songs of praise. This storied praise is captured by the word *tehillâh*.

Tehillâh is a Hebrew word meaning hymn, a song of praise, or a new, spontaneous song.

Tehillâh is a Hebrew word meaning hymn, a song of praise, or a new, spontaneous song. The book of Psalms is a collection of these kinds of songs, and in fact, in the Hebrew language, the book of Psalms is called the *Tehillum*. *Tehillâh* is a word that was used fifty-seven times in the scriptures, with over half of those occurrences being found in the psalms.

Songs of *tehillâh* may not rhyme; perhaps they don't have the catchiest tune. These songs may not be the most polished, but they come from the worshipper's heart, in the moment. Songs of *tehillâh* flow from the depths of intimacy with God.

Psalm 22:3 (NKJV) is, perhaps, my favorite use of the word *tehillâh*. It reads,

> But You are holy,
> Enthroned in the praises (*tehillâh*) of Israel.

The notion of Psalm 22:3 is beautiful. When we offer new songs of praise, our spontaneous *tehillâh*, the Lord steps from his heavenly courts and takes residency among the congregation. God inhabits their *tehillâh*, is enthroned on it.

Have you lifted a spontaneous song of praise and worship to God? Have you found yourself so overcome with his work in your personal story that you can't help but sing to him? If you haven't, consider your story, the ways God is at work in it, and lift a spontaneous song to him. Even if the words don't rhyme, even if you can't carry a tune, even if you don't know quite what to sing, practice raising a spontaneous song of praise to God. It may be awkward at first, perhaps even uncomfortable. But if you do, I know you'll find this truth: God will inhabit, incarnate your act of *tehillâh*.

BEHIND THE MUSIC
Good Good Father

I was on the road when I received a text message from Lauren. She'd been attending a women's conference in Texas, and while there, she'd heard a song that undid her. She wanted me to listen to it, the message read, and she included a link. I read the text just before leading worship, so I put my phone back in my pocket and promptly forgot about the exchange.

Days later I returned home, and Lauren met me at the door. The way I remember it, she cut to the chase pretty quickly.

"Did you listen to the song?" she asked, even before I put my bags down.

"I'm sorry. It slipped my mind."

"We're listening to it right now," she said, then began playing it on her phone. The words to the verse were beautiful and poignant, but it was the chorus that grabbed me.

> You're a good good Father;
> It's who you are.
> And I'm loved by you,
> It's who I am.

I've written my fair share of songs, and I've listened to more than my fair share. This song, though, was different somehow.

It was an invitation to the fatherly love of God, and I was so moved I grabbed my phone and Googled who'd written it. The writers, I found, were Pat Barrett and Tony Brown. I'd known Pat for some time, knew he was involved in a house church movement in Atlanta, and I emailed him to thank him for his part in bringing the song to life.

Over the following weeks, I listened to "Good Good Father" on repeat. I sang it around the house. I listened to it in the car. I taught it to my daughters and we sang it each night before bed. The song took shape in my daily life, and it became such a source of encouragement. It was an expression of praise that had pulled Lauren into it, then me, then my daughters, and the more I sang it, the more I wondered: *Couldn't it be a song of great gravity for the church?*

I reached out to Pat again, told him I'd love to record the song. He responded, said he was excited. If I wanted to record the song, though, he suggested I talk to Tony about the birth of "Good Good Father."

I'd later talk with Tony Brown on the phone and listen as he shared his incredible retelling of the song's origins. He'd been leading worship at his house church, a church of no more than fifty people. One evening, after a time of worship, one of the young ladies in the group asked for prayer. She'd had a rough season battling cancer, and despite the many prayers, healing didn't come. Their little group, Tony said, had a practice of believing that God was good, even in the hard times. So that night, they circled their wounded sister and declared the goodness of God, even while asking for healing.

Tony shared how the Spirit of God fell on the room, how thick his presence was. In that moment, with all the prayers being lifted, a chorus came to Tony and he began to sing it over his friend.

"You're a good good father. It's who you are. It's who you are."

He said he'd been apprehensive to sing the song at first. Would the chorus be frustrating to her? Would it feel hollow? But as he whispered the song in that moment, this struggling woman joined in, then the rest of the group.

"I bet we sang it for an hour," he said, "and an electricity like lightning hit the room."

Even in a moment of suffering, this band of brothers and sisters had found the goodness of God. Over the following months, the song became part of their weekly liturgy. Whenever a stress or struggle was raised, the congregants in that little house church broke into the chorus. Whenever there was pain, they sang it. That song became their lifeline, Tony said.

"I find it amazing that something as simple as a spontaneous song can unlock the most important ideas about who God is," Tony said. "I never knew my father, and I didn't meet my mother until I was twelve. So when I came to Christ, I felt like I had a father for the first time, and he was so good. I want to be an instrument of the Father's heart to people. That the song ministered the Father's heart to that woman in that moment—it was amazing."

This song that had made such an impact on my life, even in just a few months, was made even more impactful by Tony's story. But still, I couldn't imagine the impact it would come to have on the church as I stepped into the studio to record it. I didn't know it'd take root in churches across the country, that it'd spread from community to community like a house fire. I didn't know it'd be downloaded by millions.

"Good Good Father" is a song that's connected the world to God as a good father, and it was a new song, a song of spontaneity born in the heart of a man who never knew his earthly father. It's an expression of *tehillâh* that might seem ironic given the circumstances, but it's not. Instead, it's a perfect expression of the perfect ways of the good good Father.

Six: The Songs of Praise
FOR REFLECTION AND DISCUSSION

Praise is the rehearsal of our eternal song. By grace we learn to sing, and in glory we continue to sing.

—CHARLES HADDON SPURGEON

Read the following verses:

Psalm 40:3

Psalm 33:3

Psalm 144:9

Revelation 14:3

Revelation 5:9

Ephesians 5:19

Matthew 26:26–30

Personal and group reflection questions:

1. Based on these verses, how important do you think the worship practice of singing was in the ancient world?

2. Do you ever sing new, unrehearsed songs to the Lord? What does this practice do in your heart?

3. Read the quote by Charles Haddon Spurgeon. Do any words or phrases stand out to you? How do these words impact the way you think about praising God?

4. Which worship songs have been most meaningful to you?

5. What environment is your favorite place to praise God?

seven

THE SHOUT
OF PRAISE

שָׁבַח

SHABACH

Shâbach, shaw-bakh´: To address in a loud tone. To shout. To commend, glory, and triumph.[9]

One generation shall praise (shâbach) Your works to another, And shall declare Your mighty acts.

—PSALM 145:4 NKJV

Brandy and I started our family in the shadow of the windy city, and though it was a great place and we were part of an amazing church, over time, we felt God calling us to contend for the future of the American church. We felt led to give the next several decades of our lives to the next generation, to plant a new church in a new city. Which city? That minor detail wasn't quite so clear.

During a time of family prayer, I told our daughters we were considering leaving Chicago to plant a church. They asked the normal questions: *Where? When?* We told them we didn't know, but we declared our trust in God. We'd go wherever he sent us. And in the meantime, as crazy as it all seemed, we'd praise him for what he'd do.

Weeks later, we put our house on the market. Our neighbors asked the same questions: *Where are you moving? When?* I didn't know, I told them, but we were sure God would lead us. And in the meantime, we'd praise him.

We sold the house within months, and as the moving company loaded our boxes, they asked where we were moving. I told them, too, that I didn't know.

Honestly, I felt like a madman, unsure where this trust in God would take us. Brandy and I were stepping out, declaring our faith in both our actions and words, and we were giving our children a front row seat to the madness.

Ultimately, God made his plan for our family clear, and we moved to Nashville, Tennessee. We learned that Nashville is home to more than one hundred thousand college students with 60 percent choosing to stay in the area after graduation.

Shâbach, our final Hebrew word of praise, means to address in a loud tone, to shout, to commend, to glory, or to declare triumph.

Our children joined us in this journey of uncertainty and faith. They've seen how God led and provided for us, how he's done so many miraculous things in our lives. They've seen how we've raised a shout of praise for everything he's done. And it's my hope that when they're adults, when they're making their own decisions, they'll remember those shouts of praise. It's my hope that when culture shouts at them, when it asks them to reject their faith and to conform, they'll drown out those siren songs with their own declarations of faith, trust, and praise. It's my hope that they'll raise a *shâbach.*

Shâbach, our final Hebrew word of praise, means to address in a loud tone, to shout, to commend, to glory, or to declare triumph. Quite literally, it means to raise a holy roar. The word is used sparsely in the Old Testament, a mere eleven times, but each time, it has powerful effect.

In Psalm 63, David penned a song of praise while he was in the wilderness of Judah. He wrote:

> You, God, are my God,
> earnestly I seek you;
> I thirst for you,
> my whole being longs for you,
> in a dry and parched land
> where there is no water . . .
> Because your love is better than life,
> my lips will glorify you.
> I will praise (*shâbach*) you as long as I live,
> and in your name I will lift up my hands.
> (vv. 1, 3–4)

Even in the dry places, the desert places, David resolved to live out his days by lifting a shout of praise to God.

This shout of praise, this *shâbach*, is not simply a personal declaration though. The shortest psalm, Psalm 117, calls all nations to raise a holy roar. In the simplest *shâbach* found in all of Scripture, the psalmist wrote:

> Praise the LORD, all you nations.
> Praise (*shâbach*) him, all you people of the earth.
> (v. 1 NLT)

The most vivid "cultural *shâbach*" that I have ever seen happened recently. It was a gathering of more than five million people. It was reported as the seventh largest gathering in human history. At one point, that crowd gave a full-bodied, full-volume shout at the top of their lungs. It was a thunderous sonic boom. It was a unified colossal roar.

The location? Hutchinson Field in Grant Park in downtown Chicago. The occasion? The Chicago Cubs winning the Major League Baseball World Series.

As a former resident of Chicago, I can appreciate how Cubs fans have lamented 108 years without a World Series victory. Entire generations of Chicagoans have been born, grown up next to Wrigley Field, lived long lives, and died without ever seeing the Cubs win it all. This was a shout that represented a century of pent-up anticipation and disappointment.

This corporate celebration, this shout, gives us the clearest image of *shâbach*. Every time we gather with God's people to praise him, one voice unites with another. Songs become anthems. Anthems become declarations. Declarations become a holy roar.

The notion of *shâbach* transcends geography; it's a holy roar that reaches from one generation to the next. In Psalm 145:4 (NKJV), the psalmist wrote:

> One generation shall praise (*shâbach*) Your works
>   to another,
> And shall declare Your mighty acts.

The holy roar of praise is not self-contained, not just for a particular people in a particular space. It's not praise for the purpose of pumping up the present crowd. It's for the purpose of passing on the faith from one generation to the next. The next generation, the future church, is waiting for the sound of *shâbach*.

The shout of praise needs your voice. Join the holy roar.

BEHIND THE MUSIC
How Great Is Our God

I was in my loft apartment in Austin, reading Psalm 104. I was meditating on the passage, and as I did, I was overcome by the expressions of God's greatness recorded by the psalmist.

> LORD my God, you are very great;
>   you are clothed with splendor and majesty.

The LORD wraps himself in light as with a garment;
he stretches out the heavens like a tent
and lays the beams of his upper chambers on their waters.
(vv. 1–3)

I considered the power of the poetry, and as I did, a simple melody came. Then came the chorus.

How great is our God.
Sing with me, how great is our God.
All will see how great,
How great is our God.

At first I thought it might be too simple, too straightforward. But as I sang it, I began to incorporate phrases from the psalm. The song built and built, and when I'd finished composing it, I felt I had something special. Could it be an anthem of God's greatness? Could it be a holy roar?

"How Great Is Our God" became a staple of my worship sets in the months that followed, and each time I sang it, I was filled with such gratitude, such awe of the greatness of God. I recorded the song, began taking it on the road with me, and as I did, I noticed churches around the country began singing it. The song spread and spread, and quickly it became my most sung song. It became part of modern hymnbooks and had been downloaded millions of times. How far had it spread, though? I had no idea.

Years later, I was recording my album *Hello Love* alongside producer Ed Cash. "How Great Is Our God" was the first song Ed produced for me, and he'd been the one to suggest the addition of the bridge—"Name above all names, worthy of all praise, my heart will sing how Great is our God." (A pretty good suggestion, I'd say.) On one particular day, as I stepped into the studio, I got word that the Watoto Children's Choir, a choir of orphans from Uganda, was visiting Nashville. Ed and I had already spoken about including a children's choir on one of the tracks, and this group would be more than perfect. So I reached out to their director and asked if they could join us in the studio.

"Any chance you guys could record a song with us?" I asked.

"Yes," the director responded. "We have one day off, and it happens to be tomorrow."

I took it as a sign of divine intervention. The following day, we were all in the studio together. I'd heard them sing before, knew how incredible they were, but in that setting, I could see on their faces that they were nervous. I wondered whether they could see it on my face. I was nervous too.

Standing in another room of the studio, headphones on, I heard the director say to the choir, "Let's warm up. Let's sing something comfortable." There was a pause, and the children stood straighter. They gathered their breath and broke into chorus.

> How great is our God.
> Sing with me, how great is our God.

It was a beautiful moment, and their voices rang clear. They sang the chorus again and again, and my eyes began to water.

Did these orphans from the other side of the world have any idea I'd written that song?

No chance.

This eruption of praise, this shout, is the true essence of praise. It is a holy roar.

Tears began to roll down my cheeks, and as I watched them, I wondered just how this anthem had crossed the ocean. A song I'd written in the privacy of an Austin studio apartment had made its way to an orphanage in Uganda.

How great is our God.

This song has become an international anthem. Why has it left such an impression on the church? I wish I knew. Perhaps it's because the song isn't about what God's done for us; it's simply about who he is. When we gather in praise to make him greater, when we empty ourselves, doesn't it do something unlike anything else? I've come to understand that by now.

Every time I sing this song, I look forward to the moment when the congregation sings the bridge, the moment we declare that Jesus is the "name above all names." I can almost feel faith washing over the people, and I watch as some raise their hands, some fall on their knees, and some simply stand, crying. It's a moment when the people so often lead *me* in praise, when they remind *me* that I am a part of this living *shâbach*. I sing through the end, play the last chord, and listen as the crowd erupts in shouts of praise to God. This eruption of praise, this shout, is the true essence of praise. It is a holy roar.[10]

FOR REFLECTION AND DISCUSSION

Oh, can You hear it?
It's the song of the redeemed
The pursuit of passion for the One who set us free
Oh, can You hear it?
We're crying out for more
Listen to our song
It's turning into a Holy Roar.
—NATHAN AND CHRISTY NOCKELS

Read the following verses:

Psalm 98:4

Psalm 71:23

Psalm 35:27

Psalm 66:1–2

Psalm 95:1

Joshua 6:20

Ezra 3:11

Isaiah 12:6

Personal and group reflection questions:

1. Based on these verses, how common do you think the practice of a "shout of praise" was in the ancient world?

2. Do you regularly worship God with a shout of praise?

3. Read the lyrics from "Holy Roar" by Nathan and Christy Nockels. Do any words or phrases stand out to you? How do these words impact the way you think about praising God?

4. Have you ever been in an environment where you were part of a loud corporate shout of praise?

5. Think about or describe that scene. How did you feel in that moment?

conclusion

THE PRACTICE
OF PRAISE

Seven times a day I praise you
for your righteous laws.
Great peace have those who love your law,
and nothing can make them stumble.

—PSALM 119:164–165

Some time ago, I went with some friends to a U2 concert. These friends were good Christian folks of the more reserved worshipping variety. As we stood in the stadium, we belted the tunes of our childhood—"With or Without You" and "Where the Streets Have No Name." In that moment, I was transported back to the eighth grade, and there I was with my best mates, acting quite undignified. My friends, these fellas who were not expressive in church, were just as undignified as I was, and they were raising their hands and jumping up and down. We were selling out.

After the show, I considered the energy of my friends and wondered what had gotten into them. Why could U2 songs elicit such expression, such foolishness? In church, when they sang about Jesus—his life, death, and resurrection—when they sang about their own freedom, what was keeping them from offering just as much enthusiasm? Shouldn't they be even more effusive in those moments of praise?

I thought, too, about the power of the moment, the camaraderie we felt at that concert. We came together for one purpose: to celebrate the music of U2. It was a unifying moment, a moment we'll never forget.

This is what wholehearted, full-bodied praise does (even in a non-sacred context). It brings people together in unity.

This truth was embodied by the Israelite people, a people known for tribal divisions, for factions, for internal backbiting. Despite all their differences though, the entire family of the Israelites made a pilgrimage to Jerusalem three times a year, and on their way to the temple, they sang the same songs, the psalms of ascent. The psalms of ascent culminate in a final, unifying declaration of praise before the King. Psalm 134 (NLT) reads,

> Oh, praise (*bârak*) the LORD, all you servants of the LORD,
> you who serve at night in the house of the LORD.
> Lift your hands toward the sanctuary,
> and praise (*bârak*) the LORD.
> May the LORD, who made heaven and earth,
> bless you from Jerusalem.

Can you imagine the people joining together, completely unified in their act of praise as they make their way to the temple?

There can be no doubt—unity is found when we praise the Lord together. When believers in King Jesus gather together to ascend to his throne, denominational divisions and disunity disappear. Baptist, Methodist, Catholic, nondenominational, whatever—we show our family unity when we lift our unabashed, unbridled, full-bodied praise. We incarnate Jesus's prayer that we would be "one." What believer doesn't want that?

I suppose that begs the question: What keeps us from joining together as one body and fully expressing our praise to King Jesus?

There can be no doubt—unity is found when we praise the Lord together. When believers in King Jesus gather together to ascend to his throne, denominational divisions and disunity disappear.

I remember when I was first starting on this (accidental) journey into ministry twenty years ago. I'd only been a pastor for a short time when I wondered whether we should dial things back in our worship gatherings. I wondered whether our expressions of worship should be more subdued so that visitors wouldn't be weirded out. But even as I was trying to justify these questions to God, I felt the Holy Spirit rebuking me, asking me if I genuinely thought the greatest way to represent the joy of Jesus was to offer a sterile version of worship. Did I really think a room full of people standing stiff as ironing boards would somehow draw the world in? Wouldn't the most unifying expression of praise be authentic and unashamed?

I repented. I turned back into the fullest expression of worship I knew. I was determined to grow in that expression. I haven't turned back since.

As you read this book, perhaps you found yourself outside of your comfort zone on occasion. Maybe you were uncomfortable with the notion of lifting your hands to God, of dancing, kneeling, or raising a shout. Perhaps you couldn't see yourself singing a spontaneous song to God. Maybe it was a little too charismatic, too expressive. If you found yourself feeling this way, know this: It's okay. God knows where you are, even though he wants you to grow in your expression of praise to him. But know this too: God wants your full, free expression of praise. He says as much over and over again in the scriptures. And his desire for your praise isn't contingent on our personalities, our feelings in the moment, our comfort zones, or whether or not we're mired in some unshakable sin. As noted by Richard J. Foster, the question isn't what sort of worship makes you comfortable or will meet your need, but "What kind of worship does God call for?" Foster writes:

Often our "reserved temperament" is little more than fear of what others will think of us, or perhaps unwillingness to humble ourselves before God and others. Of course, people have different temperaments, but that must never keep us from worshipping with our whole being.[11]

Worship, see, is an imperative. It's required. It's a whole-being daily practice.

In Psalm 119:164, David wrote, "Seven times a day I praise you for your righteous laws." No matter where he was, who he was with, or what he had to do, he made space to praise God. And if David were to walk into your modern life, if he were to visit you in the coffee shop, or climb into your cherry-red Mazda RX-7, what would you observe about his praise practices? You might note how he'd stop midconversation and ask for a moment to offer praise to God. He might fall on his knees, or raise his hand, or shout right there in the coffee shop: "God, you are so good!" It wouldn't be a one-time practice. Seven times a day you'd experience this kind of interruption from David. He'd ask you to pull over so he could kneel on the side of the road. He'd ask you to drive him to the church building so he could offer some new song of praise. Your friends might look at him as if he were crazy, might ask you why your friend David was always dancing or kneeling or shouting or singing in praise. You'd shrug your shoulders and look to him. He'd just laugh and say, "You think this is abnormal? 'I will become even more undignified than this because of what God has done for me. He's set me free!" (see 2 Samuel 6:22).

David, the king of all of Israel, the great unifier of the people—we could all learn so much from his indignities.

The seven Hebrew words of praise—*yâdâh, hâlal, zâmar, tôwdâh, bârak, tehillâh,* and *shâbach*—have changed the way I enter God's courts. In them, I've found complete freedom to express my praise to God.

The seven Hebrew words of praise—*yâdâh, hâlal, zâmar, tôwdâh, bârak, tehillâh,* and *shâbach*—have changed the way I enter God's courts. In them, I've found complete freedom to express my praise to God. My guess is, if you explore the depths of these words, if you take them to heart, you'll find that freedom too, and you'll become a living expression of praise.

Come with us on this unifying journey of praise.

Join the *shâbach* of God's people.

Become a part of the holy roar.

Conclusion
FOR REFLECTION AND DISCUSSION

Worship at its best is a social experience with people of all levels of life coming together to realize their oneness and unity under God. Whenever the church, consciously or unconsciously caters to one class it loses the spiritual force of the "whosoever will, let him come" doctrine, and is in danger of becoming little more than a social club with a thin veneer of religiosity.
—MARTIN LUTHER KING JR.

Read the following verses:

Psalm 133
Romans 15:6
Philippians 2:2
1 Peter 3:8
Acts 2:1
Colossians 3:14

Personal and group reflection questions:

1. Based on these verses, how important do you think unity is within the church community?

2. Music style is sometimes a divisive factor in churches. How could you use it to produce unity?

3. Read the quote by Martin Luther King Jr. Do any words or phrases stand out to you? How do these words impact the way you think about praising God?

4. How is your church community doing with "all levels of life" coming together? Is this something you are actively working toward?

5. If praising God in a corporate gathering is a practice of unity, how can you work to cultivate a greater degree of unity in your church?

APPENDIX

Songs and their lyrics have been central to the content and themes of *Holy Roar*. We are thankful to the following for permission to reprint portions of them here.

"GOD'S GREAT DANCE FLOOR"
Written by Chris Tomlin, Martin Smith, and Nick Herbert

Copyright © 2013 Thankyou Music (PRS) (adm. worldwide at CapitolCMGPublishing.com excluding Europe which is adm. by Integrity Music, part of the David C Cook family. Songs @integritymusic.com) / Worship Together Music (BMI) sixsteps Songs (BMI) S.D.G. Publishing (BMI) Gloworks Limited (PRS) (adm. at CapitolCMGPublishing.com) All rights reserved. Used by permission.

"GOOD GOOD FATHER"
Written by Pat Barrett and Anthony Brown

Copyright © 2014 Common Hymnal Digital (BMI) Housefires Sounds (ASCAP) Tony Brown Publishing Designee (BMI) worshiptogether.com Songs (ASCAP) sixsteps Music (ASCAP) Vamos Publishing (ASCAP) Capitol CMG Paragon (BMI) (adm. at CapitolCMGPublishing.com) All rights reserved. Used by permission.

"HOLY IS THE LORD"

Written by Chris Tomlin and Louie Giglio

Copyright © 2003 worshiptogether.com Songs (ASCAP) sixsteps Music (ASCAP) Vamos Publishing (ASCAP) (adm. at CapitolCMGPublishing.com) All rights reserved. Used by permission.

"HOLY ROAR"

Written by Christy Nockels and Nathan Nockels

Copyright © 1996 Rocketown Music, LLC., Word Music, LLC, and Sweater Weather Music (adm. Word Music Group, Inc.) All rights reserved. Used by permission.

"HOW GREAT IS OUR GOD"

Written by Chris Tomlin, Jesse Reeves, and Ed Cash

Copyright © 2004 worshiptogether.com Songs/sixsteps Music /ASCAP (adm. @ CapitolCMGPublishing.com)/Alletrop Music /BMI All rights reserved. Used by permission.

"I LIFT MY HANDS"

Written by Chris Tomlin, Louie Giglio, and Matt Maher

Copyright © 2010 Thankyou Music (PRS) (adm. worldwide at CapitolCMGPublishing.com excluding Europe which is adm. by Integrity Music, part of the David C Cook family. Songs @integritymusic.com)/worshiptogether.com Songs (ASCAP) sixsteps Music (ASCAP) Vamos Publishing (ASCAP) Valley Of Songs Music (BMI) (adm. at CapitolCMGPublishing.com) All rights reserved. Used by permission.

NOTES

1. Martyn Lloyd-Jones, *Walking with God Day by Day: 365 Daily Devotional Selections*, ed. Robert Backhouse (Wheaton, IL: Crossway, 2013), 164.

2. Richard J. Foster, *Celebration of Discipline* (New York: HarperCollins, 1998), 168.

3. "3034. יָדָה **yâdâh**, *yaw-daw'*; a prim1. root; used only as denom. from 3027; lit. to *use* (i.e. hold out) *the hand*; phys. to *throw* (a stone, an arrow) at or away; espec. to *revere* or *worship* (with extended hands); intens. to *bemoan* (by wringing the hands):— cast (out), (make) confess (-ion), praise, shoot, (give) thank (-ful, -s, -sgiving)." James Strong, *A Concise Dictionary of the Words in the Greek Testament and The Hebrew Bible, Volume 2* (Bellingham, WA: Logos, 2009), 47.

4. "1984. הָלַל **hâlal**, *haw-lal'*; a prim. root; to *be clear* (orig. of sound, but usually of color); to *shine*; hence to *make a show*, to *boast*; and thus to *be* (clamorously) *foolish*; to *rave*; causat. to *celebrate*; also to *stultify*:—(make) boast (self), celebrate, commend, (deal, make), fool (-ish, -ly), glory, give [light], be (make, feign self) mad (against), give in marriage, [sing, be worthy of] praise, rage, renowned, shine." Strong, *A Concise Dictionary of the Words in the Greek Testament and The Hebrew Bible, Volume 2*, 33.

5. "2167. זָמַר **zâmar**, *zaw-mar'*; a prim. root [perh. ident. with 2168 through the idea of *striking* with the fingers]; prop. to *touch*

the strings or parts of a musical instrument, i.e. *play* upon it; to make *music*, accompanied by the voice; hence to *celebrate* in song and music:—give praise, sing forth praises, psalms." Strong, *A Concise Dictionary of the Words in the Greek Testament and The Hebrew Bible, Volume 2*, 35.

6. "8426. תּוֹדָה **tôwdâh**, *to-daw'*; from 3034; prop. an *extension* of the hand, i.e. (by impl.) *avowal*, or (usually) *adoration*; spec. a *choir* of worshippers:—confession, (sacrifice of) praise, thanks (-giving, offering)." Strong, *A Concise Dictionary of the Words in the Greek Testament and The Hebrew Bible, Volume 2*, 123.

7. "1288. בָּרַךְ **bârak**, *baw-rak'*; a prim. root; to *kneel*; by impl. to *bless* God (as an act of adoration), and (vice-versa) man (as a benefit):—× abundantly, × altogether, × at all, bless, congratulate × greatly, × indeed, kneel (down), praise, salute, × still, thank." Strong, *A Concise Dictionary of the Words in the Greek Testament and The Hebrew Bible, Volume 2*, 24.

8. "8416. תְּהִלָּה **tehillâh** (239d); from 1984b; *praise, song of praise*:—praise(47), praises(6), praising(1), song of praise(1)." Robert L. Thomas, *New American Standard Hebrew-Aramaic and Greek Dictionaries : Updated Edition* (Anaheim: Foundation Publications, 1998), #.

9. "7623. שָׁבַח **shâbach**, *shaw-bakh'*; a prim. root; prop. to *address* in a loud tone, i.e. (spec15.) *loud*; fig16. to *pacify* (as if by words):—commend, glory, keep in, praise, still, triumph." Strong, *A Concise Dictionary of the Words in the Greek Testament and The Hebrew Bible, Volume 2*, 111.

10. For copyright information for "How Great Is Our God" and the other songs discussed in this book, see the appendix.

11. Foster, *Celebration of Discipline*, 170.

ACKNOWLEDGMENTS

A huge thanks to Seth Haines who worked tirelessly to help us write and edit this book. Thanks to Micah Kandros for the cover design. Thanks to Jocelyn Bailey for line editing and Mandi Cofer for the page design.

CHRIS THANKS

Our Savior, Jesus . . . to him be the glory.

My wife, Lauren, and daughters, Ashlyn and Madison . . . I love my beautiful girls and you have forever changed my life in every good way.

Anthony Piedmonte and Jessi Shadden at Piedmonte & Co. I could not keep anything straight without your incredible help. Thank you for your hard work behind the scenes.

My band and crew that keeps the music and the road a gift.

Grateful for the people all over the world who have shared so many moments with me and my music. I continue to pray that these songs help you connect with our great God.

DARREN THANKS

Jesus, I have nothing but gratitude. You alone deserve the praise. Dum Spiro Spero.

Brandy, Sydney, Scarlett, and Violet, thanks for your grace and patience with me as we worked on this! There's nothing better than sharing life with my girls.

Jon Tyson, my Aussie mate for over twenty-five years. Thanks for your support and for sharing the research on the seven Hebrew words for praise.

Julie Shiffert, my executive assistant, thanks for handling everything!

Chris, thanks for believing in this project. How improbable and crazy was this story? #progress

Joel Edwards and the Evolve team. You guys are amazing! Preston Cannon and Jeff Goins for sharing your expertise.

The *Church of the City* family, being a part of this church community is the joy of my life.

ABOUT THE AUTHORS

CHRIS TOMLIN

With eleven albums, sixteen #1 radio singles, a Grammy Award, twenty-one Dove Awards, and two platinum and five gold albums to his credit, Chris Tomlin is among the most well-known and influential artists in music. His songs include "How Great Is Our God," "Amazing Grace (My Chains Are Gone)," "Our God," and most recently "Good Good Father," to name a few. It is estimated that each week twenty to thirty million people sing one of Tomlin's songs in worship. More than anything, Chris loves being a husband to Lauren and a dad to Ashlyn and Madison.

christomlin.com
twitter *@christomlin*
Instagram *@christomlin*

DARREN WHITEHEAD

Originally from Australia, Darren Whitehead founded Church of the City in Nashville, Tennessee, in 2013. Each weekend more than five thousand people worship at one of the four locations across the metro area. Prior to this, Darren served at Willow Creek Community Church in Chicago, Illinois, as a teaching pastor for eight years. Darren earned his master's in ministry and is currently completing his doctorate. He lives with his wife, Brandy, and their three daughters, Sydney, Scarlett, and Violet in Nashville, Tennessee.

churchofthecity.com
twitter *@darrenwhitehead*
Instagram *@darrenwhitehead*